Staging Gender

Unmasking Butler's Performativity Paradigm

The Curious Philosopher

Copyright Page

Disclaimer

The views and opinions expressed in this book are those of the author(s) and do not necessarily reflect the official policy or position of any other agency, organization, employer, or company. The contents of this book are for informational and educational purposes only and are not intended to serve as professional advice, diagnosis, or treatment.

The information provided in this book is believed to be accurate and reliable as of the date of publication. However, it may include some errors or inaccuracies, and no warranty or guarantee is provided regarding the accuracy, timeliness, or applicability of the content.

Readers are encouraged to consult with professional philosophers, educators, or other qualified professionals where appropriate for personalized advice. The author(s) and publisher shall not be liable for any loss, damage, or harm caused or alleged to be caused, directly or indirectly, by the information or ideas contained, suggested, or referenced in this book.

By reading this book, the reader acknowledges and agrees that they
are solely responsible for how they interpret and apply the information contained herein.

This book may also include references to other works, studies, and
sources. These references are provided for further reading and exploration and do not imply endorsement or validation of the specific
theories, viewpoints, or interpretations presented in those works.

Chapter 1: Introduction - Stepping onto the Gender Stage

A Tale of Two Shirts

Imagine walking into a store and seeing two shirts. One, blue with a picture of a robot and the label "For Boys." The other, pink with a unicorn and labeled "For Girls." Why are they separated like this? Why can't a girl like robots or a boy like unicorns? It's questions like these that plunge us into the world of gender, how it shapes us, and how we shape it.

Why is Gender So Important?

You might wonder, why does gender even matter? It's just a label, right? But the reality is, from the moment we're born and sometimes even before that, our gender becomes one of the most defining aspects of our lives. It dictates the clothes we wear, the toys we play with, the jobs we might have, and even how we're expected to behave.

Consider this: why are boys generally encouraged to be "strong" and "tough," while girls are often nudged towards being "gentle" or "kind"? Why is a man who shows emotion sometimes seen as "weak," while a woman who asserts herself can be labeled "bossy"? It's all because of societal expectations tied to gender.

And that's just scratching the surface. Gender plays a role in how we're paid, how we're treated, and even how we see ourselves. So, understanding gender is not just about challenging pink shirts and blue shirts; it's about creating a world where everyone feels seen, valued, and free to be themselves.

Enter Judith Butler: A New Lens on Gender

Imagine thinking of gender not as something we are but as something we do. This is where Judith Butler, a philosopher and gender theorist, enters our story. While most of us grew up with the idea that there are two distinct genders, male and female, and that they're determined by our biology, Butler introduced a groundbreaking idea.

She suggested that gender isn't just about biology. Instead, it's like a performance, a series of actions and behaviors that we've learned over time, much like a role in a play. Every day, through our choices and behaviors, we "act out" our gender, following a script society has handed us. But what if we could change the script?

Butler's Significance: Shaking the Gender Tree

Butler's ideas were revolutionary. By suggesting that gender is performative, she opened the door for challenging strict gender roles. If gender is a performance, then it means it's flexible and can change. It means that the boy who wants to wear the pink shirt with a unicorn can do so without fear. It means that we all have the power to redefine what it means to be male, female, or any other gender identity.

Moreover, her work laid the foundation for countless activists, scholars, and ordinary people to question, challenge, and ultimately reshape society's understanding of gender. And as we'll see in this book, the impact of her theory stretches far and wide, from classrooms to courtrooms, from homes to workplaces.

The Journey Ahead

Understanding gender might seem like a daunting task. There's so much to unpack, so many questions to answer. But don't worry; you're not alone on this journey. Together, we'll dive into the world of gender performance, challenge long-held beliefs, and, hopefully, come out with a more inclusive and flexible understanding of what it means to be human.

Chapter 2: The Story of Gender – From Fixed Ideas to Flexible Thoughts

The "Pink is for Girls, Blue is for Boys" Mentality

Remember when we talked about pink shirts for girls and blue shirts for boys? This idea didn't just pop out of nowhere. For a long time, people believed that the way you acted as a male or female was set in stone, determined by nature itself. This belief is what we call Essentialism.

Essentialism: Born This Way?

Essentialism is like saying, "Boys are naturally like this, and girls are naturally like that." It's the idea that men and women have certain 'essences' or core qualities that are innate and unchangeable. Think of it as baking a cake: Essentialism says that the ingredients (or traits) that make up men and women are fixed, and you can't change the recipe.

For a long time, many people accepted this. They believed that biology – our genes, hormones, and physical bodies – determined everything about our gender. But as time went on and societies evolved, some started to question this "fixed recipe" idea.

Social Constructivism: Maybe It's Not All About Biology?

Enter the game-changer: Social Constructivism. This theory says that our understanding of gender isn't just based on biology. Instead, it's shaped by society, culture, and our environment. In other words, society has a huge hand in teaching us how to "be a man" or "be a woman."

Imagine if, from the day you were born, everyone around you insisted that the sky was green. Even if you saw it as blue, you'd probably start believing it was green because everyone said so. That's how powerful society can be in shaping our beliefs and behaviors. And that's what Social Constructivism highlights – that our ideas of gender are learned, not just something we're born with.

Setting the Stage for Butler: When Two Worlds Collide

As thinkers and scholars wrestled with these ideas, two major movements were on the rise: Feminist Theory and Post-Structuralism.

Feminist Theory, in simple terms, is the study of women's rights and the challenges they face in society. It looks at how women have been treated differently (and often unfairly) compared to men and seeks ways to address that.

On the other hand, Post-Structuralism is a bit trickier but think of it as a way of understanding the world that says there's no single "truth." Instead, everything is open to interpretation, and many factors shape our understanding of concepts like gender.

Now, imagine these two ideas having a deep conversation. That's what happened in the world of gender studies. The questions raised by feminists met the flexible thinking of post-structuralists, creating a vibrant mix of ideas. And right in the middle of this mix was Judith Butler, who took inspiration from both to craft her groundbreaking theory of gender performativity.

Wrapping It Up: The Story So Far

Gender isn't just about whether you're male or female. It's a complex mix of biology, society, and personal experience. We started with the idea that everything was set in stone (Essentialism). Then, we realized society played a huge role in shaping our gender (Social Constructivism). And now, with thinkers like Butler, we're exploring the exciting idea that gender can be like a performance, ever-changing and fluid.

As we continue this journey, we'll dive deeper into these ideas and explore how they impact our daily lives.

Chapter 3: Performativity – Life's Unseen Theater

The Everyday Stage

Picture this: You're at a grand theater, the curtains rise, and actors appear, performing their roles with perfection. Now, what if I told you that this theater is everywhere and you're one of the actors? Every day, without even realizing it, we're all 'performing' in the grand play of life. And the role we often find ourselves acting out? Gender.

So, What's Performativity Anyway?

Performativity might sound like a big, fancy term, but at its heart, it's a simple concept. Think of it as the idea that we don't just have a gender; we do our gender. It's not just something we are, but something we express through our actions, behaviors, and choices every single day. It's like a dance we've been taught since birth, where we move in ways that society expects based on whether we're seen as male, female, or another gender.

Speaking of Gender: The Power of Words

Have you ever been told to "man up" or "act like a lady"? These aren't just words; they're commands, instructing us how to behave based on our gender. These kinds of phrases, which we can call "speech acts," play a big role in shaping our gender performances.

For instance, when a baby boy is constantly told that "boys don't cry," he learns to hold back his tears, even if he feels like crying. On the flip side, a girl told to "sit properly" learns to be cautious about how she occupies space. Over time, these speech acts mold our actions, making us conform to society's expectations.

Everyday Rituals: More than Just Habits

Apart from the words we hear, there are also countless little 'rituals' we follow. Think about the way boys might be encouraged to play with trucks while girls with dolls. Or how men might be nudged towards wearing pants and women towards dresses. These rituals, practiced again and again, reinforce society's gender rules.

Butler's Wake-Up Call: Questioning the 'Stable' Identity

Butler took a magnifying glass to these performances and asked a simple yet powerful question: Why? Why do we stick to these fixed roles and behaviors? Why can't gender be more flexible?

She pointed out that the idea of having a 'stable' gender identity – where everyone fits neatly into boxes of 'male' or 'female' – is limiting. It's like being handed a script at birth and being told, "This is your role. Don't deviate." But what if you don't like the script? What if it doesn't feel right?

Butler argued that we should be free to rewrite our scripts, to define our own gender without society's constraints. After all, if gender is a performance, shouldn't we have the freedom to choose our roles?

Taking the Stage: A New Way of Seeing Gender

By understanding performativity, we start to see the world in a new light. We recognize the invisible theater around us and how we've been cast in roles that we didn't always choose. But the most empowering realization? We have the power to change the script.

In the upcoming chapters, we'll explore how this idea of performativity has challenged old norms and sparked movements, allowing people everywhere to express their true selves.

Chapter 4: The Script of Gender – Life's Invisible Lines

Imagine Life as a Play

Have you ever been to a play? The actors, following their scripts, bring characters to life, each line rehearsed and each movement practiced to perfection. Now, what if I told you that outside the theater, in our daily lives, we too are following a script, especially when it comes to gender?

The Invisible Scripts We Follow

From the moment we're born, society hands us a script. If you're a boy, your script might read: "Be tough, don't show emotions, aspire to be strong." If you're a girl, it might say: "Be gentle, be caring, look pretty." These scripts, or societal norms, dictate how we should behave, what we should like, even what we should aspire to be – all based on our gender.

You might remember the pink and blue shirts from before. That's a simple example of the script in action. But it goes much deeper, influencing our choices, our behaviors, and even our dreams.

Rehearsing Without Realizing: Society's Training Regime

But how do we end up following these scripts so diligently? It's through a process of what we can call "unconscious rehearsal."

Think back to when you were a child. Perhaps you were a boy given trucks to play with, while your sister was given dolls. Or maybe you were a girl told to sit with your legs crossed, while your brother sprawled out however he liked. Over time, these small nudges, these unconscious rehearsals, train us into our gender roles.

It's like practicing for a play you didn't even know you were a part of. Every "Boys don't do that" or "It's not ladylike" is a director's instruction, steering us back to our scripted roles.

The Chains of Rigid Scripts: The Side Effects

While some might argue that these scripts provide structure, they can also be confining, even harmful. Here's why:

Limited Potential: By telling a girl she shouldn't pursue math because it's "for boys," we limit her potential. By telling a boy he shouldn't dance because it's "feminine," we stifle his passion.

Emotional Strain: When men are constantly told to "man up" and not show emotion, it can lead to emotional suppression, which isn't healthy. Similarly, when women are expected to always be nurturing and caring, it can lead to burnout.

Identity Crisis: For those who feel their gender doesn't fit neatly into the 'male' or 'female' box, these scripts can be suffocating. They might feel lost, forced into roles that don't resonate with who they truly are.

Turning the Page: Rethinking Our Scripts

Understanding that we've been handed a script is the first step to freedom. By recognizing these societal norms, we can start to question them. Why should girls like pink? Who said boys can't cry?

While these scripts have been rehearsed over generations, it doesn't mean they can't be rewritten. As we'll see in the chapters ahead, breaking free from these confining scripts can lead to a richer, more authentic life where everyone gets to be the star of their own show.

Chapter 5: Resisting and Reshaping – The Colorful World of Drag

A Stage Unlike Any Other

Imagine a stage shimmering in glitter, powerful music playing, and out steps a dazzling performer. With sky-high heels, a flawless makeup look, and an outfit that would make anyone turn heads. This isn't just any stage; this is the world of drag. But while it's entertainment for many, drag offers a profound insight into the way we think about gender.

Drag: More Than Just a Show

At first glance, drag might seem like just a fun performance, but it's also a thought-provoking critique of gender. Remember the scripts we talked about? Drag artists, through their performances, question these very scripts.

When a drag queen amplifies feminine traits, using exaggerated makeup or mimicking stereotypical female behaviors, she's not just putting on a show; she's highlighting how society has constructed these ideas of "femininity." It's like holding up a magnifying glass to our gender expectations, showing us how constructed and even sometimes absurd they can be.

The Parody and Power: Unmasking Gender

The beauty of drag is its ability to parody gender. By taking the expected traits of masculinity and femininity and amplifying them, drag performers showcase how fluid and performative gender really is. It's a reminder that, just as they are putting on a persona for the stage, many of us put on a gender persona in our daily lives, often without realizing it.

But there's power in this parody. By playing with gender norms, drag artists show us that these norms aren't as fixed as society makes them out to be. It's a bold statement, saying, "Look, I can switch between genders, play with them, and redefine them. So can you."

Challenging the Status Quo: The Reveal Behind the Glitz

Drag doesn't just entertain; it educates. By stepping onto the stage and playing with gender expectations, drag artists challenge societal norms. They show us that gender is not just what we're born with, but something we do, perform, and can redefine.

To put it simply, drag exposes the "act" of gender. It reminds us that, just like a drag artist can switch from their everyday identity to a stage persona, our everyday gender roles are also a switchable, changeable act.

Stepping Out of the Shadows: The Legacy of Drag

The impact of drag extends beyond the stage. By challenging and reshaping our ideas of gender, drag has paved the way for many to embrace their true selves, outside the confines of societal norms. It's a celebration of individuality, a nod to the rebels, and an invitation for all of us to question, reshape, and even discard the scripts we've been handed.

In the chapters to come, we'll dive deeper into the individuals and movements that have been inspired by this drag paradigm, pushing boundaries and rewriting the rules of the gender game.

Chapter 6: Tackling the Waves – Implications, Cheers, and Jeers

A Whisper, then a Roar

Imagine dropping a stone into a calm pond. At first, there's a small splash, then ripples start to spread, reaching every corner of the water. Judith Butler's ideas on gender performativity had a similar effect. While initially a subtle murmur in the academic world, her theory set off ripples that spread far and wide, sparking both acclaim and controversy.

Mixed Reviews from the Home Team

The feminist community, which one might expect to be in full agreement with Butler, had a spectrum of reactions. On one hand, many hailed her ideas as groundbreaking. By suggesting that gender isn't something inherent but performed, Butler provided a fresh way to think about gender oppression and how to combat it. It gave activists a new tool in their arsenal, emphasizing that if gender norms are just societal performances, they can be changed.

However, not everyone was on board. Some feminists argued that by focusing on gender as a performance, Butler's theory could potentially undermine the very real experiences and oppressions faced by women. They worried that if gender is just seen as an act, then serious issues like wage inequality or reproductive rights might be overlooked or downplayed.

Beyond Theories: Activism in the Real World

Butler's influence wasn't just limited to intellectual debates. It spilled into real-world gender activism. By emphasizing the fluidity of gender, her work lent support to non-binary and genderqueer communities. It encouraged people to question and resist rigid gender norms, leading to more inclusive movements and campaigns.

Modern Tussles: Bathrooms, Games, and Identities

The ripple effect of Butler's work can be seen in many contemporary issues:

Bathroom Bills: The debate over who should use which restroom might seem simple, but it's deeply tied to our understandings of gender. If we see gender as fluid, as Butler suggests, then the idea of strictly male or female restrooms becomes questionable.

The Arena of Sports: Who gets to compete in women's sports? This question has stirred a lot of debates, especially concerning transgender athletes. If gender is performative and not strictly tied to biology, how should sports categories be defined?

Identity Politics: As more people identify outside the traditional male/female binary, there's been a surge in discussions about rights, recognition, and representation. Butler's theory, emphasizing the flexibility of gender, plays a significant role in these debates.

Sailing Forward: Navigating the Waters of Change

While Butler's ideas on gender performativity opened doors to new ways of thinking, they also ignited debates, controversies, and vital discussions. And that's the beauty of it. It's through such debates that societies grow, evolve, and hopefully, become more inclusive.

As we delve deeper in the chapters ahead, we'll explore how these implications have played out globally, shaping policies, cultures, and individual lives.

Chapter 7: Breaking the Mold - Beyond the Binary

The Two-Box Dilemma

Let's start with a simple exercise. Imagine you're faced with two boxes: one labeled "male" and the other "female." You're asked to fit everything about gender into one of these two boxes. Seems limiting, doesn't it?

For a long time, society functioned like this exercise, trying to fit the vast, intricate world of gender into just two boxes. But just like trying to pour the ocean into a teacup, it doesn't quite work.

Challenging the Two-Box System

The binary system of gender, which says you're either male or female, leaves no room for anyone who doesn't quite fit into those definitions. And the truth is, a lot of people don't.

This isn't just about biology; it's about identity, experience, and self-expression. By clinging to the binary, society effectively erases or invalidates the identities of countless individuals.

The Expansive Galaxy of Gender

Enter a richer understanding of gender. Just as we've come to recognize a vast universe beyond our Earth, we're beginning to acknowledge an expansive gender spectrum beyond the binary.

Non-binary: This is a general word for gender identities that don't correspond with one gender or the other. Think of it as refusing to be boxed in.

Genderqueer: This term represents those who reject traditional gender distinctions and identify as neither exclusively male nor exclusively female. It's like choosing to color outside the predefined lines.

And Beyond: Terms like genderfluid, agender, and two-spirit further showcase the diversity of gender experiences. The language of gender is evolving, offering more nuanced ways for people to express who they truly are.

Where Paths Cross: The Web of Intersectionality

But, as we talk about gender, we must recognize it doesn't stand alone. Imagine a web, where each thread represents an aspect of your identity: race, class, sexuality, ability, and more. At the center, where all these threads intersect, lies your unique experience.

This idea is known as intersectionality. It reminds us that people aren't defined by just one aspect of their identity. A Black transgender woman's experience, for example, can't be understood by looking at race, gender, or class in isolation. They're intertwined, each affecting and amplifying the other.

By understanding intersectionality, we see that gender performativity doesn't happen in a vacuum. The "scripts" we follow, and how society views us, are shaped by a complex interplay of factors.

Envisioning a World Without Boxes

While boxes can be comforting, they can also be confining. As we move forward, it's essential to keep questioning, expanding, and redefining our understanding of gender. A world without restrictive boxes isn't just more inclusive; it's more real, capturing the beautiful diversity of human experience.

Chapter 8: Small Ripples, Big Waves – Acts of Resistance and the Power of Disruption

Little Acts, Big Statements

Picture this: A boy walks into school wearing nail polish. A girl decides to play with trucks instead of dolls. Someone you know decides to use different pronouns. At first glance, these might seem like small things, mere blips in the everyday routine. But look a bit closer, and you'll see that they're much more than that.

Defying the Script in Everyday Life

Every time someone steps out of the expected gender roles, they're challenging deep-seated societal norms. That boy with nail polish isn't just expressing a fashion preference; he's saying that colors and expressions have no gender. The girl playing with trucks? She's asserting that interests and passions aren't bound by gender boxes.

These everyday acts of resistance are powerful. They're quiet reminders that gender norms are just that – norms, not rules. By disrupting these norms in daily life, individuals pave the way for broader acceptance and change.

United We Stand: The Strength of Collective Movements

However, there's also strength in numbers. Throughout history, collective movements have played a pivotal role in reshaping society's understanding of gender.

Think of the suffragettes, fighting for women's right to vote. The pride parades, championing LGBTQ+ rights and acceptance. The global campaigns against gender-based violence. These movements, made up of countless individuals uniting for a common cause, have reshaped societies, laws, and attitudes.

By coming together, individuals amplify their voices, turning quiet whispers of change into roaring demands for equality and acceptance.

The Butterfly Effect: Inspiring Acts of Change

Have you heard of the idea that a butterfly flapping its wings can cause a tornado on the other side of the world? It's a metaphor for how tiny acts can have massive, unforeseen consequences.

Similarly, acts of resistance, whether individual or collective, have ripple effects. That boy with the nail polish might inspire another boy to wear a dress to school. The girl with the trucks might encourage parents to let their children choose toys without the boundary of "for boys" or "for girls." Movements inspire other movements, stories give birth to new stories, and the cycle of change continues.

Stepping Stones to a Brighter Tomorrow

While the path to dismantling rigid gender norms is long, every act of resistance, big or small, is a step in the right direction. It's a reminder that change often starts with a single act, a single voice, a single story.

Chapter 9: Beyond Horizons – The Future of Gender in a Changing World

Setting the Scene: A Glimpse Into Tomorrow

Imagine a world where there are no pre-set roles based on your gender, where the line between male and female is not rigid but soft and fluid. Where everyone can be their authentic selves, free from societal expectations. Sounds idyllic, doesn't it? As we stand on the brink of numerous societal shifts, this vision might be closer to reality than we think.

Reading the Signs: Predictions from Today's Changes

Change is in the air. From fashion to entertainment, workplaces to homes, we're witnessing an increasing blurring of traditional gender lines. Clothes are becoming more unisex, parental roles are evolving, and spaces are becoming more inclusive.

If these trends continue, we can foresee a future where gender is viewed more as a spectrum than a binary. This doesn't mean gender will cease to exist, but rather that it'll be understood in a broader, more nuanced way. A world where each person is free to define, and redefine, their gender without societal pressures.

Virtual Realities: How Tech Shapes Tomorrow's Gender Landscape

The digital age brings with it a fresh arena for gender exploration. With avatars, online identities, and virtual realities, technology offers a sandbox for people to play with and express gender in ways that were previously unimaginable.

Online platforms and games, for example, allow individuals to experiment with gender presentation in a virtual space, challenging and expanding their understanding of gender. As technology continues to evolve, we might find digital spaces pioneering new ways of thinking about and expressing gender, breaking away from real-world constraints.

Molding Minds: The Crucial Role of Education and Policy

But for a truly inclusive future, the change has to start from the ground up. Education plays a pivotal role in shaping young minds. By incorporating inclusive gender education, schools can become breeding grounds for acceptance and understanding.

This includes teaching about diverse gender identities, challenging traditional gender norms, and fostering an environment where every child feels seen and accepted.

Moreover, policies that support gender inclusivity, be it in workplaces, public spaces, or legal systems, can lay the groundwork for a future where everyone, regardless of their gender, feels safe, respected, and valued.

Charting Uncharted Waters: The Journey Ahead

While the future of gender is uncertain, one thing is clear: it's heading towards a more fluid, inclusive frontier. With societal shifts, technological advancements, and progressive education and policies, the future looks promising.

However, it's essential to remember that the journey towards this future requires collective effort. It's a tapestry woven with threads of understanding, acceptance, and action from each one of us.

In our concluding chapter, we'll reflect on the journey we've undertaken in understanding gender, and the steps each of us can take to contribute to a brighter, more inclusive tomorrow.

Chapter 10: Turning the Page - Your Role in the Next Chapter of Gender

A Journey Revisited: The Paths We've Walked

Take a moment to reflect on our journey. From the roots of traditional gender roles to the revolutionary thoughts of Judith Butler, we've ventured deep into the intricate maze of gender. We've seen its constraints, its fluidity, its expressions, and its future possibilities.

Understanding gender isn't just an academic pursuit. It's about recognizing the unseen scripts that shape our lives, the invisible chains that can bind or free us. By critiquing these norms, we're not just gaining knowledge; we're gaining the power to shape our world.

Envisioning a World Without Barriers

Imagine a society that celebrates gender in all its shades and forms. A place where children grow up without the weight of gendered expectations, where love isn't confined by outdated norms, and where everyone can authentically be themselves.

This isn't a utopian dream. As we've seen, the wheels of change are already in motion. By embracing gender fluidity, we're not just creating a more inclusive society; we're also unlocking the potential of countless individuals who've been sidelined or suppressed by rigid gender roles.

Your Role in the Story: A Call to Action

But here's the thing: this isn't a tale written by unseen hands. It's a story we're all authoring, with our beliefs, actions, and conversations. So, what can you do?

Educate Yourself and Others: The first step to change is understanding. Read, listen, and converse. Share what you've learned with others.

Challenge the Norms: If you see rigid gender expectations playing out in your surroundings – be it in the media, at work, or in casual conversations – question them. Encourage others to do the same.

Support Inclusivity: From supporting gender-inclusive policies to standing by individuals who defy gender norms, every act counts.

Reflect and Evolve: Your understanding of gender doesn't have to be set in stone. As society evolves, so can you. Keep an open mind, and let your understanding of gender be a living, evolving entity.

The Pen is in Your Hand

In conclusion, while the chapters of this book may end here, the story of gender is ongoing. With every act of understanding, acceptance, and change, you're not just a reader but a writer, shaping the next chapter of the gender narrative.

The future is fluid, vast, and full of potential. With understanding as our compass and acceptance as our guide, there's no limit to the horizons we can explore.

About The Curious Philosopher

Welcome to The Curious Philosopher, your dedicated platform for diving deep into the world of philosophy. We are more than just a YouTube channel or a book publisher. We are a beacon of enlightenment, making complex philosophical concepts accessible and engaging for all.

Our YouTube channel is a rich repository of philosophy made simple. We take the profound and often complex ideas from the world of philosophy and break them down into digestible, easy-to-understand content. From the ancient wisdom of Socrates to the existentialist thoughts of Sartre, we cover a broad spectrum of philosophical schools and thoughts, making philosophy accessible to everyone, regardless of their background or prior knowledge.

As a book publisher, we take the same approach, transforming intricate philosophical theories into comprehensible narratives. Our books are not just collections of words, but vessels of wisdom that make philosophy approachable and relatable. We believe that philosophy should not be confined to academic circles, but should be available to all who seek to understand the world and their place in it.

At The Curious Philosopher, we believe in the power of curiosity and the pursuit of knowledge. We are here to stoke the fires of your curiosity, to guide you on your intellectual journey, and to help you navigate the fascinating world of philosophy.

If you are someone who is not afraid to question, to explore, and to learn, then you are in the right place. Join us on this journey of exploration, as we make philosophy easy to understand, one concept at a time.

Be sure to visit our Youtube channel at:

https://www.curiousphilosopher.com/youtube

You can also visit us on the web at

https://www.curiousphilosopher.com

Welcome to The Curious Philosopher. Stay curious. Stay enlightened.